D1518639

Black Caiman

by Ellen Lawrence

Consultant:

Stephen Hammack
Herpetarium Keeper
St. Louis Zoo
St. Louis, Missouri

New York, New York

Credits

Cover, © Gabriel Rojo/Nature Picture Library; 4T, © belizar/Shutterstock; 4B, VladSer/Shutterstock; 5, © Manado/iStock; 6, © Cosmographics; 7, © Gabriel Rojo/Nature Picture Library; 8, © Nature Picture Library/Alamy; 9, © Toni Sánchez Poy/Alamy; 10T, © Wrangel/iStock; 10B, © N_u_T/Shutterstock; 11, © Michael & Patricia Fogden/Minden Pictures/FLPA; 12, © Toni Sánchez Poy/Alamy; 13, © DEA/G. Sosio/Getty Images; 14, © James Caldwell/Alamy; 15, © Luiz Claudio Marigo/Nature Picture Library; 16, © Luiz Claudio Marigo/Nature Picture Library; 17, © Mark MacEwen/Getty Images; 18, © Luiz Claudio Marigo/Nature Picture Library; 19, © Pete Oxford/Nature Picture Library; 20T, © Andre Dib/Shutterstock; 20B, © Patrick K. Campbell/Shutterstock; 21, © Kymri Wilt/Danita Delimont/ardea; 22 (L to R), © Toni Sánchez Poy/Alamy, © Franco Banfi/Biosphoto/FLPA, © Carlos Aguilera/Shutterstock, and © Tom Stack/Alamy; 23TL, © Glenn Young/Shutterstock; 23TC, © Ondrej Prosicky/Shutterstock; 23TR, © alexeys/iStock; 23BL, © Filipe Frazao/Shutterstock; 23BC, © Matt Jeppson/Shutterstock; 23BR, © dangdumrong/Shutterstock.

Publisher: Kenn Goin
Senior Editor: Joyce Tavolacci
Creative Director: Spencer Brinker
Photo Researcher: Ruby Tuesday Books Ltd

Library of Congress Cataloging-in-Publication Data

Names: Lawrence, Ellen, 1967– author.
Title: Black caiman / by Ellen Lawrence.
Description: New York, New York : Bearport Publishing Company, Inc., [2017] |
   Series: Apex predators of the amazon rain forest | Audience: Ages 5–8. |
   Includes bibliographical references and index.
Identifiers: LCCN 2016044534 (print) | LCCN 2016050326 (ebook) | ISBN
   9781684020324 (library) | ISBN 9781684020843 (ebook)
Subjects: LCSH: Caimans—Juvenile literature. | Alligators—Juvenile
   literature.
Classification: LCC QL666.C925 L3935 2017 (print) | LCC QL666.C925 (ebook) |
   DDC 597.98/4—dc23
LC record available at https://lccn.loc.gov/2016044534

For more information, write to Bearport Publishing Company, Inc., 45 West 21st Street, Suite 3B, New York, New York 10010. Printed in the United States of America.

10 9 8 7 6 5 4 3 2 1

Contents

Hidden Danger 4

Watery World 6

Meet a Black Caiman 8

Huge Hunters 10

Night Predator 12

Time to Build a Nest 14

A Devoted Mom 16

Tiny in a Big World 18

King of the Amazon 20

Science Lab 22

Science Words 23

Index 24

Read More 24

Learn More Online 24

About the Author 24

Hidden Danger

It's early evening in the Amazon **rain forest**.

A tapir comes to a river to drink.

The tapir doesn't realize that danger is lurking just a few feet away.

Floating in the dark water is a giant black caiman.

Still and silent, the hungry **predator** watches the tapir— and then attacks!

tapir

black caiman

Caimans are related to alligators and crocodiles.

Watery World

Black caimans live in parts of South America, including the Amazon rain forest.

They make their homes in ponds, lakes, and large rivers.

These creatures also live in smaller rivers that flow through the Amazon.

Often, they rest among the plants that grow along muddy riverbanks.

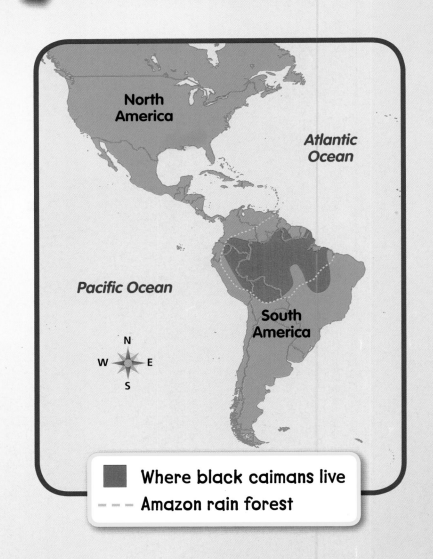

North America

Atlantic Ocean

Pacific Ocean

South America

N
W   E
S

■ Where black caimans live
- - - Amazon rain forest

Black caimans also live in areas known as wetlands. In a wetland, shallow water covers the ground.

Look at this picture of a caiman. Can you think of five words to describe the animal?

Meet a Black Caiman

Black caimans are huge!

They can grow to be 16 feet (4.9 m) long—or about the length of a pickup truck.

Most adult caimans weigh about 200 pounds (91 kg).

Some big males, however, can weigh up to 800 pounds (363 kg)!

Caimans' giant bodies are covered with thick black **scales**.

scales

webbed foot

A caiman has webbed feet for swimming. It also has a long powerful tail that it swishes from side to side to move through water.

tail

Huge Hunters

Black caimans aren't picky eaters.

They will eat whatever they can capture and kill.

Caimans often hunt for fish, including catfish, perch, and piranha.

Huge snakes, such as anacondas, and turtles also make up part of their diet.

Black caimans can easily crunch through a turtle's shell with their powerful jaws and teeth.

catfish

Amazon river turtle

Caimans also hunt animals that live on land, such as monkeys, sloths, and wild pigs. They often grab these animals when they come to rivers or ponds to drink.

a caiman eating a fish

How do you think a caiman's dark skin helps it when it's hunting?

11

Night Predator

A black caiman usually hunts at night.

Its black skin blends in with the dark water, helping it to sneak up on its **prey**.

After it attacks, it swallows fish and other small animals whole.

If it catches a large animal on a riverbank, the caiman drags its meal into the water.

Then it holds its struggling prey underwater until the animal drowns.

a caiman blending in with dark water

Caimans can't chew their food. If an animal is too big to swallow whole, a caiman stores its meal on a riverbank. Once the flesh starts to rot and soften, the caiman then tears off chunks to eat.

chunk of meat

13

Time to Build a Nest

Every two to three years, an adult female caiman is ready to have babies.

After **mating** with a male caiman, she finds a place on a riverbank to build a nest.

First, she digs a shallow hole in the mud with her back feet.

Then she lays up to 60 eggs in the hole.

Finally, she covers her eggs with a huge mound of leaves, twigs, and mud.

a caiman looking for a place to build a nest

Do you think a mother caiman guards her eggs or abandons them?

These scientists are examining a caiman's nest.

The leaves and twigs in the caiman's nest rot and produce heat. The heat helps the baby caimans grow inside their eggs.

eggs

A Devoted Mom

A mother caiman fiercely guards her nest. Why?

Raccoons, snakes, and other animals love to eat caiman eggs.

After about two months, the baby caimans hatch.

When the mother hears them chirping, she helps dig them out of the nest.

If a baby gets stuck in its egg, she gently breaks the eggshell with her big teeth.

a baby caiman hatching

Sometimes a mother caiman carries her babies in her mouth.

Tiny in a Big World

The baby caimans are tiny—just 6 to 8 inches (15 to 20 cm) long.

Predators, such as snakes, large birds, fish, and even other caimans, try to eat them.

To keep safe, the babies stay close to their mother.

They also stick together in a group called a pod.

a pod of baby black caimans hiding among water plants

King of the Amazon

As the young caimans grow bigger, they have fewer predators.

Once they are a few feet long, their only enemies are giant anacondas and jaguars.

As a fully grown adult, a caiman has no predators.

With its tough skin and large, powerful body, the black caiman is the apex, or top, predator in the Amazon!

jaguar

green anaconda

Black caimans are cold-blooded **reptiles**. A reptile's body temperature changes when the air or water around it heats up or cools.

Science Lab

Comparing Amazon Predators

Black caimans aren't the only huge predators that live in the Amazon River.

Choose one of the hunters below and use books and the Internet to research how it lives and hunts.

Next, make a chart like the one shown here to compare and contrast a black caiman with another predator you've chosen.

Black Caimans and Electric Eels

Things that are the same:	Things that are different:
• Both animals live in the Amazon River in South America.	• A black caiman is 16 feet (5 m) long, and an electric eel is half that size.
• Black caimans and electric eels both hunt and eat fish.	• Electric eels stun or kill their prey with electricity. A caiman bites or drowns its prey.

Black Caiman
16 feet (5 m)

Green Anaconda
17 feet (5.2 m)

Bull Shark
11 feet (3.4 m)

Electric Eel
8 feet (2.4 m)

Science Words

mating (MAYT-ing) coming together to produce young

predator (PRED-uh-tur) an animal that hunts other animals for food

prey (PRAY) an animal that is hunted and eaten by another animal

rain forest (RAYN FOR-ist) a large area of land covered with trees and other plants where lots of rain falls

reptiles (REP-tilez) cold-blooded animals, such as lizards, snakes, and caimans, that have scaly skin

scales (SKAYLZ) tough, overlapping sections, or plates, on a reptile's skin

Index

Amazon rain forest 4, 6, 20
baby caimans 14–15, 16–17,
    18–19, 20
eggs 14–15, 16
food 10–11, 13, 19, 22

hunting 4, 10–11, 12–13, 19, 22
mating 14
mother caimans 14, 16–17, 18–19
nests 14–15, 16
prey 4, 10–11, 12–13, 22

reptiles 21
scales 8
skin 8, 11, 12, 20
swimming 8–9
wetlands 7

Read More

Baxter, Bethany. *Caimans, Gharials, Alligators, and Crocodiles (Awesome Armored Animals).* New York: Rosen (2014).

Heos, Bridget. *What to Expect When You're Expecting Hatchlings: A Guide for Crocodilian Parents (and Curious Kids).* Minneapolis, MN: Lerner (2012).

Lawrence, Ellen. *American Alligator (Swamp Things: Animal Life in a Wetland).* New York: Bearport (2017).

Learn More Online

To learn more about black caimans, visit
www.bearportpublishing.com/ApexPredators

About the Author

Ellen Lawrence lives in the United Kingdom. Her favorite books to write are those about nature and animals. In fact, the first book Ellen bought for herself, when she was six years old, was the story of a gorilla named Patty Cake that was born in New York's Central Park Zoo.